LESLEY M. KAYE

Chatting with the Universe

MY COSMIC DIARY

Channeling for a new understanding
of your life and ways, and the truth of reality

All rights reserved; no part of this book may be reproduced, stored in a retrieval system, or transmitted, in any form or by any means, without the prior permission in writing from the publisher, nor be otherwise circulated in any form of binding or cover other than that in which it is published and without a similar condition, including this condition being imposed on the subsequent purchaser.

First published in Great Britain in 2023 by Quill Literature

Copyright © 2023 by Lesley M. Kaye
Editorial Services by Marsha D. Phillips
Cover Design and Typesetting by Arjan van Woensel

ISBN: 978-1-7397426-2-1

The moral right of the authors has been asserted.

Nothing in this book is to be taken as professional medical advice and is the opinion and experience of the authors. The authors and publisher accept no liability for damage of any nature resulting directly or indirectly from the application or use of any information contained within this book. Any information acted upon from this book is at the reader's sole discretion and risk.

First Edition

Divine channel to the Universe, I dedicate this book to you. May the illuminated words you write bring you heartfelt love and joy.

INTRODUCTION

Welcome to *Chatting with the Universe: My Cosmic Diary*, a companion to *Diary of a Scribe to the Universe: A Cosmic Accord*. May this diary start an exciting inward journey!

When scribing — or channelling written messages — feel free to ask any question you would like answered. This is your space and time, and there is no right or wrong question to ask, just as there is no right or wrong way to scribe. If the process feels strange at first, don't worry, with time it will feel more natural. You may find that your ability to hear messages is affected by how you feel, what's on your mind, or things you need to do. Below are some tips to help you begin this wonderful experience.

....
The Ritual of Channelling
....

When
Set aside time to channel, in the morning or evening — whenever feels best for you — the choice is yours and will depend on how you feel at certain times of the day and your daily commitments. If possible, select a time you will not be disturbed by others or your phone, or have other possible interruptions.

Where
Find a specific place to scribe. If you do not have a writing area available at present, do your best to create one. If this isn't possible, make sure you feel comfortable where you choose to scribe.

How
I have found that the first and best approach to channelling is to relax. Choose an activity that brings you calm and peace of mind, such as lighting a candle and watching the flame, playing gentle music,

spending time in nature, or meditating. It may also help to imagine yourself in a large bubble of light. I like white light, generally, but let the right colour come to you. Also, choose a pen or pencil that you like.

Take 3 deep breaths. This is your signal to spirit that you would like to make contact. Don't forget to keep taking nice deep, relaxed breaths. When you feel relaxed, write your question and wait for your reply. It might arise as words you hear in your mind, or feelings, such as happiness or peacefulness; or physical sensations, such as warmth, coolness, or tingles. Alternatively, you may receive images. Make a note of these as they are your response. All of these, or a combination of them, is possible. If you do not receive a reply, it's okay, you can try again another time.

If you receive images or shapes and feel you would like to draw them, try the *Art with the Universe: My Cosmic Canvas* and begin to create.

Whatever form your message comes in, it is perfect! The most important thing is to enjoy the experience. This is a special communication just for you, so do what feels right, what brings you happiness. The more you honour what you are given, the more you will understand its meaning.

Questions

If you have never channelled written messages before, you may want to use some of the questions I started with, such as:

Who am I?
Who are you?
Why are we here?
Tell me about the significance of life on Earth.

Or, you may feel more comfortable with:

Is there anyone with a message for me?
What is my message for today?

Alternatively, you may prefer to start a sentence and see how it is finished.

Sentence Starters

Below are a few examples you can use to open up to spirit and invite a message.

Hello and welcome,
I am so happy to hear...
My message for today is...

However you decide to start your channelled message, here is a piece of advice Yahvay gave to me:

'Ask the questions that your heart burns with desire to hear the answers to, for they are the most pressing of matters.'

Don't forget to look at the companion publications in the Lesley M. Kaye with Yahvay collection:

Diary of a Scribe to the Universe: A Cosmic Accord
On This Day of Days: Daily Messages of Love and Wisdom

Art with the Universe: My Cosmic Canvas
Journalling with the Universe: My Divine Conversations (unlined)
Let Your Sparkle Sparkle: Ponder and Power Cards
Let Your Sparkle Sparkle: Desk Calendar

Further details for all these publications can be found at www.quill-literature.co.uk

By far, the most important thing is to have fun. Enjoy. Happy scribing!

Lesley

About Lesley M. Kaye

Having spent most of her working life in education, Lesley is now semi-retired apart from teaching some Italian. She lives in England with her family and three rescue cats. Along with a passion for channelling and all things spiritual, Lesley also loves nature, languages, art, crystals, music, property programmes and reading.

Channelling has now become a wonderful way of life for Lesley. This passion extends to encouraging others to channel for themselves to discover the love and wisdom of the Universe on their own personal journey.

www.ingramcontent.com/pod-product-compliance
Lightning Source LLC
Chambersburg PA
CBHW072053110526
44590CB00018B/3153